Worlds to Explore

Junior Badges and Signs

Girl Scouts of the U.S.A.
830 Third Avenue
New York, N.Y. 10022

Inquiries related to *Worlds to Explore: Junior Badges and Signs* should be addressed to the Program Department, Girl Scouts of the U.S.A.

Contents

Junior Girl Scout Insignia

Insignia are those official symbols that you wear on your uniform. Your Girl Scout pin and the World Association pin are the most important insignia. There are also insignia Girl Scouts earn.

In Brownies you and your troop may have worked on Brownie B Patches. As a Junior Girl Scout, you can explore even more interests through badges, signs, and the Junior Aide Patch.

A badge is about one subject, while a sign explores many subjects. Like badges, signs have requirements. Juliette Low said that every badge you earn is related to our motto, "Be Prepared." She explained that a badge is not a reward or a medal; it is something you have done so often and so well you can teach it to someone else.

A sign is an invitation to action. For some parts of a sign you might earn a badge. For other parts, you might help to carry out another kind of project, such as doing something for your community, going on a trip, or making a film. Each sign has its own symbol. When you complete the requirements you can wear it on your uniform sash as a reminder of your adventures and accomplishments.

There is also a Junior Aide Patch. It indicates that you participated in helping Brownies to cross the bridge to Junior Girl Scouts.

Placing Insignia on Your Uniform

Most insignia go on the front of your badge sash. Look at the sash in the picture to see where to sew or pin on each piece of insignia. (Patches from events, camp, or special projects may be sewn on the back of the sash.) You may wear your sash as soon as you become a Junior Girl Scout. You add to it the insignia you earn as a Junior.

When you become a Cadette, badges you earned as a Junior are sewn onto the right side of the Cadette vest. Cadette badges are worn on the left side. Cadette badges have gold borders where Junior badges are green.

Junior Girl Scout Badges

There are over 40 badges that Junior Girl Scouts can earn. Each badge is about a different subject. You have dozens to choose from. You can even make up a badge of your own.

Each badge has its own requirements. These are the things you will need to do to earn the badge. Each requirement is a way to find out about, to try, or to practice something about the subject you have chosen. With your troop leader's help, you can change some badge requirements if you want to make the badge more fun or more useful to you.

Help with badge requirements is scattered all through *Worlds to Explore: Handbook for Brownie and Junior Girl Scouts.* You will find that many badges are related to more than one of the Worlds. For example, things you must know to earn the Backyard Fun Badge are in both the "World of Well-Being" and the "World of the Out-of-Doors." The My Camera Badge can take you into the "World of Today and Tomorrow" as well as the "World of the Arts." Try the index of your *Worlds to Explore* book before looking anywhere else for the information you need.

Most often, you work on badge requirements with a small group of friends who are all interested in the same badge subject. Sometimes you earn a badge that no one else has chosen. Visiting different places, making things, meeting people, teaching others what you have learned can all be part of the fun of earning a badge.

For each badge you earn, there is a badge symbol you can wear on your uniform sash. It shows you have new knowledge and skills that you can use and share with others.

Keep a record of your badge work by having your leader (or another person chosen by you and your leader) fill in the blank beside each requirement as soon as you finish it. You may do part of a badge at camp. You might even move to another place and another troop before you complete a badge. If you keep a record in this book, you and your troop leader will decide when you have earned a badge. When you have done each requirement and you and your troop leader agree that you have met the purpose of the badge, you have earned the badge.

Badges are presented at a ceremony called Court of Awards. Then you sew your badges on your badge sash. Your troop may want to have a Court of Awards as soon as most of you have earned your first badges. Or you may wait and have a big Court of Awards. Invite guests and have all the badges earned by the troop presented.

Some steps you can take to choose and earn badges are:

1 Pick a subject that interests you—one that is new to you or one that you would like to learn more about.

2 Look through the "Badge Requirements" section to find badges with activities about your subject.

You can't find badges covering your subject? If you and others in your troop have an interest that the badges don't cover, you can create a new badge of your own. For "how to," see the Our Own Troop's Badge, page 62.

3 When you find some badges that fit your interest, read the badge purpose and requirements carefully. Choose the badges you would like to earn and decide which one you want to do first.

4 Seek out others in the troop who would like to earn the same badges as those you have chosen. If no one else shares your interest ask your leader if you can work on your own.

5 With your leader's help join forces with girls who want to earn the same badge. Find an adviser who will help you as you earn this badge. An adviser can be:

    your troop leader,

    a parent or teacher,

    a Cadette or Senior Girl Scout,

    someone else who knows the badge subject.

6 Talk over these points:

How do the badge requirements help you meet the purpose of the badge?

Which requirements sound like fun?

Do any requirements sound dull or boring? which ones? why?

What are some interesting ways to do each requirement?

7 Then decide:

Which requirements will be done as written?

Will you rewrite any requirements? which ones? why?

Should any requirements be dropped? if so, why?

Will you add any requirements? what will they be?

What are your goals, and how will you know when you have successfully earned the badge?

Badge
Requirements

You will find the requirements for all the Junior Girl Scout badges on the following pages. Read the purposes of many badges before you decide which one you want to work on. The purpose tells you what you will be able to do when you have earned the badge.

Active Citizen

Purpose: To find out about and put into practice the responsibilities of a citizen of the United States of America.

When you complete a requirement, have leader initial and date it.

1 Show how to use and care for the flag of the United States. Plan and carry out a flag ceremony.

2 Explain how a person becomes a citizen of the United States, and how a person may lose citizenship.

3 Act out ways the Girl Scout Law can help you carry out the responsibilities of a citizen.

4 Discover things your family has helped to pay for in your area by paying taxes. What responsibilities do you have when you use these things?

5 Find out about some of the government agencies that serve you and your family. Visit one of them.

OR look up three local laws governing such things as bicycles, fire burning, pets, dumping. Find out why these laws were made and how they serve everyone.

6 Think about and discuss how you and your family used these freedoms during the past weeks: freedom of religion, freedom of speech, freedom of the press, freedom of assembly.

7 Plan ways that your troop could help adults get people to vote.

My signature

Leader's signature   Date badge completed

Art in the Round

Purpose: To make sculpture from different materials.

When you complete a requirement, have leader initial and date it.

1 Choose four materials from the following list and find out what kind of equipment and other supplies are needed to work with each: clay, paper-mache, soft wood, wire. Prepare sculpture material.

2 Show that you know how to care for and use materials and equipment chosen in No. 1.

3 Make something out of each of your four materials: animal or storybook characters, interesting shapes, mobiles, or stabiles.

4 Visit a museum, gallery, studio, or other place where sculpture in different materials is exhibited.

5 Make one finished piece of sculpture designed for a certain place, purpose, or person. Use one or a combination of the materials in the above list.

6 Display your art in the round at a troop meeting or at an exhibit.

My signature

Leader's signature   Date badge completed

Backyard Fun

Purpose: To learn and practice the things you need for outings in yards and parks.

When you complete a requirement, have leader initial and date it.

✔**1** Help your family, patrol, or other group plan and carry out three outings. Help prepare two different sites. Use family, troop, or public equipment such as outdoor stoves, picnic tables, fireplaces.

MAD

✔**2** Plan one meal or snack that needs no cooking, one that lets each person cook, one that you cook for a group. Help plan, buy, pack, carry, prepare, and serve the food. Help clean up.

MAD

✔**3** Make a piece of equipment such as a <u>sit-upon</u>, vagabond stove, emergency fuel, litterbag for family car, or <u>toasting fork</u>.

MAD

✔**4** Show you can make a fire, use it, put it out, and leave the fire site in good condition.

MAD

✔**5** Help plan, assemble, and pack equipment for a first aid kit.

MAD

✔**6** Come to each of the outings in No. 1 dressed for the expected weather and for activities planned.

MAD

✔**7** Get acquainted with six natural things—tree, insect, animal, flower —you find on your outings. Do an outdoor good turn that will attract and protect birds or animals, or that will help plants or trees to grow.

MAD

✔**8** Make a leaf print, track cast, sketch, or photograph of something you find outdoors.

MAD

✔**9** Include games, songs, campfires in your outings.

MAD

10 List the things you have learned to do for this badge that will be useful to you when you go on your next outing.

MAD

Kim Reinhard

My signature

Marlene Dorman

Leader's signature

3/2/81

Date badge completed

18

Books

Purpose: To find out about different kinds of books, how to use them, and how to care for them.

When you complete a requirement, have leader initial and date it.

1 With the help of someone who knows books, make a reading plan to use in the library in your school or community.

MD 1/5

2 Read three different kinds of books: adventure, biography, history, hobby, mystery, poetry, science fiction, short stories, or travel.

MD 1/5

3 For your troop make an exhibit of books about an activity you are working on, such as nature or arts.
OR prepare for the troop a list of books that would be useful in troop activities.

MD 1/5

4 Visit your school or public library to find out how to: Find a book through the card catalog. Use reference books to find answers to questions. Find magazine articles about special subjects. Use dictionary and encyclopedia. Find the publisher and price of a certain book.

MD 1/5

5 Show your troop or patrol illustrations from several books you like. Explain why you like the illustrations.

MD 1/5

6 Know how to care for books and how to mend them when necessary. Demonstrate your knowledge on your own books, help a librarian, or collect and repair books to share with others.

MD 1/5

7 Tell how books were made in the days before printing.
OR make a bookplate for your own book collection.
OR bind a book.

MD 1/5

Kim Reinhard
My signature

Marlene A Dorman
Leader's signature

1/5/81
Date badge completed

Collector

Purpose: To start, or add to, a collection of things you like and to arrange that collection so it will be interesting to others.

When you complete a requirement, have leader initial and date it.

1 Start a collection or add to one you have already started. Tell how you can collect things without disturbing the environment.

2 Figure out a way to arrange your collection at home. Use scrapbooks, shelves, boxes, or whatever seems best for the collection.

3 Group or label the objects in your collection so they will be interesting to other people.

4 Choose three objects and write a display label for each telling such things as: where you found it, age of object, how it was made, a story about it.

5 Find out more about your collection in one of the following ways: Visit another collector to see his or her exhibit. Read books and magazines. Talk to someone who knows about what you are collecting.

6 Show your troop or patrol your newest addition and one of your favorite pieces in your collection.

7 Display your collection at a troop meeting or hobby show, or invite some troop members to see your collection.

My signature

Leader's signature   Date badge completed

Community Safety

Purpose: To discover how your community protects its citizens and to do your part to make it safe.

When you complete a requirement, have leader initial and date it.

1 Know four services in your community or state that protect you and your family. Visit a branch of one of these. Learn what it does and how to call for aid in an emergency.

2 List safety practices to follow on a hike and follow them on a neighborhood hike.

OR ask the police department or other community group to help you plan a bicycle safety inspection and skills test for cyclists in your neighborhood.

3 Make and post safety rules for your playground, yard, troop meeting place, community center, or swimming pool. Observe these rules yourself and be a good example for younger children.

4 Describe an accident that has happened and discuss with others how this accident might have been prevented.

5 Discuss: The right things to do if you are approached by a stranger. Safety steps to take with discarded refrigerators and large plastic bags. How to call the nearest poison control center in an emergency.

6 Organize and carry out with others a home or neighborhood safety project, using safety facts you have learned.

My signature

Leader's signature

Date badge completed

Cook

Purpose: To learn how to cook so you can fix meals for your family.

When you complete a requirement, have leader initial and date it.

1 Show how to measure dry, liquid, and solid ingredients. Know measuring equivalents.

2 Demonstrate how to: control stove top burners, preheat an oven, clean a stove safely, and use five cooking tools.

3 With your patrol list the names and meanings of ten cooking and food terms that are new to you. Find out the basic four food groups and know why each is important to you. Plan four menus using the four food groups.

4 Show that you know how to "clean up as you go" in cooking and how to store food.

5 Find recipes from at least three different countries using a common food like beans, rice, or potatoes. Prepare one of the recipes.

6 Bake muffins, biscuits, or a quick bread.

7 Learn how to prepare the following foods and use them in planning meals: one starchy and one leafy vegetable as a side dish, one fresh vegetable salad, one cooked fruit dessert, one fresh fruit for breakfast, white sauce or a milk dessert, and two main dishes: one using meat or fish; one without meat using cheese, eggs, and/or beans.

8 Learn how to use three kinds of cereal products in meals, and prepare a dish using one of them.

9 Describe three well-balanced lunches you enjoy.

10 Plan and prepare a simple, well-balanced dinner for your family or patrol.

My signature

Leader's signature   Date badge completed

Cyclist

Purpose: To know how to ride a bicycle safely so you can take bicycle trips.

When you complete a requirement, have leader initial and date it.

1 Show that you can do these things on a bicycle: start, stop, use brake to control speed, balance yourself easily, ride at slow speed, steer, circle, and give proper signals.

2 Know and follow traffic rules. Know licensing regulations in your community. Know the parts of your bicycle and how to spot-check for safety. Know how to keep your bike clean, rust-free, and well lubricated. Know where to get your bicycle repaired. Know how to chain and lock your bicycle for safekeeping.

3 Show how to carry gear on your bicycle safely.

4 With others show how to make a shelter using ponchos and bicycles.

5 Ask an experienced cyclist to discuss with you steps to take in caring for and riding a bicycle on a bicycle trip or in planning for a bicycle trip.

6 With your patrol or small group, plan an all-day bicycle trip. Use a road map that shows alternate routes. Explain why you chose the route you did. Whenever possible, use a designated bicycle path.

7 Know some different kinds of bicycles and when each kind is most useful.

8 With your troop, patrol, or other group, plan and carry out a troop, school, or community safety project.

My signature

Leader's signature   Date badge completed

Dabbler

Purpose: To make different kinds of arts with your hands.

When you complete a requirement, have leader initial and date it.

✓**1** Paint a picture illustrating a favorite story, song, or poem.
OR paint something you like to do.
OR paint a picture of one of your friends.

✓**2** Make a small bowl or figure out of clay.

3 Invent a design and use it to make a stencil, woodblock, or linoleum block.
OR make a transfer print or monoprint.

4 Make a hand puppet of a character from a favorite story. Put on a skit using puppets.

5 Carve a toy, animal, or decoration in wood.

6 Make a small basket out of grass, pine needles, cornhusks, or other basket material you find.

✓**7** Weave something simple on a cardboard loom or some other loom you like.

8 Make a picture on heavy cloth using yarn and embroidery stitches, pieces of material, trimmings.

✓**9** Make a collage, mobile, or paper sculpture.

_____
My signature

_____
Leader's signature   Date badge completed

Dancer

Purpose: To know how to dance with other people and to learn about different kinds of dancing.

When you complete a requirement, have leader initial and date it.

1. With others learn to dance four American folk dances and four from other countries where there are Girl Guides and Girl Scouts.

2. Learn a folk dance that has ballroom steps such as a polka or a waltz. Practice with others.
OR know the names of and show how to do any eight dance steps or positions.

3. With your patrol or other interested girls, discover two musical works based on dance rhythms. Play music from these works for your troop or play recordings of the music.

4. With others make up actions to go with music you like.
OR invent some dance steps for characters from a story or a play.

5. With others find out about the history of dancing in the United States.
OR be able to tell others about the life of a famous dancer.

6. With others make costumes for folk dancing.
OR find and exhibit pictures of musical instruments used to accompany dancing in different parts of the world.

7. With others learn three singing games and teach them to a group of Brownie Girl Scouts.

My signature

Leader's signature

Date badge completed

Drawing and Painting

Purpose: To draw and paint your own collection of pictures.

When you complete a requirement, have leader initial and date it.

1 Choose any four materials from the following list: charcoal, crayon, finger paint, pencil, poster paint, watercolor. Find out what supplies and equipment are necessary to work with each of the four you choose.

2 Show that you know how to care for, clean, and store your equipment.

3 Experiment with mixing colors and using them in a painting. Experiment with such techniques as string painting, crayon etching, chalk sketching, sponge painting.

4 Use each of the materials you chose in No. 1 to paint or draw one picture. Pictures can show how you feel or can be about things you enjoy such as trips, friends, pets, camping, holidays, sports, plays, or stories.

5 Display your collection of drawings and paintings at a troop meeting, or invite some troop members to see your collection.

6 Show how to "fix" a charcoal or pencil drawing so that it will not smear.

7 Visit a museum, gallery, studio, or other place where paintings and drawings are exhibited. Tell why you like certain pictures best.

8 Select one of your pictures to mount for your home or to share with someone else.

My signature

Leader's signature

Date badge completed

Folklore

Purpose: To learn about American folk music, folk tales, and hand arts, and how they tell some of our country's history.

When you complete a requirement, have leader initial and date it.

1 Find out about the history of the people of your community—how things happened, legends and stories, early arts, songs, or dances. Tell or write a story about this history.

2 With your troop or patrol, work out a play or puppet show based on one of the legends. Include simple costumes, scenery, music, and dances.

3 Act out one of the folk songs.
OR learn one of the folk dances and teach it to others.

4 Find out all you can about arts practiced in your part of the country. Make up a notebook or file about works of early crafts-people and toys made by the people in early settlements. If possible, visit someone who can tell about or show you arts typical of your area. Using ideas from these early arts, create your own design using plant, metal, clay, wood, weaving, or embroidery.

5 Find out about the folk art in two areas other than your own: New England, Pennsylvania, Appalachian Mountains, South, Ozarks, Midwest, Northwest, Southwest, California, Alaska, Hawaii, Puerto Rico. Collect pictures or make sketches that show what you have learned.

6 With your troop or patrol, find a way to share what you have learned with others in your community. Some ways might be a book, a skit, an exhibit demonstration, or a slide show.

My signature

Leader's signature   Date badge completed

Foot Traveler

Purpose: To become a good hiker, able to take care of yourself and the trails you follow.

When you complete a requirement, have leader initial and date it.

1 Earn the Gypsy badge.

MAD

2 With your patrol, troop, camp unit, or family, plan and go on four walking trips: three at least two miles long and one at least five miles long. Three trips should be on trails or in open country. Plan routes, get necessary permissions, come dressed for expected weather and kind of hike.

3 Get together your own hike kit with drinking cup, eating utensils, compass, jackknife, rope, sit-upon.

4 Show you understand ecology by the way you use trails.

5 Plan and pack a well-balanced, easy-to-carry lunch for each hike. On one hike prepare a hot drink using a Buddy burner or other emergency fuel. On another, cook two things. Leave sites clean.

6 Whip and hank your own rope. Show that your knife is in good condition. Use at least two kinds of knots on your hikes.

7 Use a compass to follow or lay a trail on one hike. On another hike use a street or road map. Make a sketch map of a third hike, or part of it.

8 Know how to bandage an injured ankle. Know what to do in a hike emergency.

9 Know four songs or read four poems about the out-of-doors.
OR know four games to play outdoors.
OR discover four things in nature that are new to you.

_____
My signature

_____
Leader's signature

3/2/81

Date badge completed

28

Gypsy

Purpose: To be able to plan and go on an all-day hike.

When you complete a requirement, have leader initial and date it.

1 Help your patrol, troop, or camp unit plan and go on two all-day hikes. Plan where to go, what to wear and to take. Get necessary permissions and find out about fire-building regulations.

MAD

2 Know how to walk and rest correctly, how to walk in a group on street, highway, or country road.

3 Use good outdoor manners: on the way, at hike site, on trails. Do an outdoor good turn on each hike.

4 Plan and carry your lunch for one hike and cook part of it yourself. On the other hike prepare a meal for a group.

5 Help make and use: fireplace, charcoal fire, or tin can stoves.

6 Dress for expected weather and activities. Have rope, eating utensils, and bandana.

7 Learn one new campcraft skill: how to tie knots, handle a knife, use a compass, or lay and follow a trail.

8 Be able to teach a game to play on the way. Know a hiking song.

9 Help keep troop first aid kit ready for use. Know what to do if you cut or burn yourself.

10 Watch a sunset, look wide around a hilltop, or discover something interesting in nature. Find a poem or a story about the out-of-doors or about the way it makes you feel to share with your patrol.

11 After each hike, talk over the hike and what you need to learn or practice before your next outing.

Kim Reinhard

My signature

Marlee A Dorman

Leader's signature

3/2/81

Date badge completed

29

Health Aid

Purpose: To learn how to help take care of yourself and others when there is sickness or an accident.

When you complete a requirement, have leader initial and date it.

✓**1** Make a home telephone card for doctor, ambulance, police, fire department, poison control center, and other emergency calls. Keep it by the phone. In your troop, practice making proper calls, giving necessary information, and following directions.

✓**2** Practice five ways to help when someone is sick in your home.
OR demonstrate the proper use and care of a hot water bottle, heating pad, and ice bag.

3 With three or four others, demonstrate the things you would do to be sure of comfort and safety on a hike.

4 Demonstrate first aid for: fainting, small cuts, blisters, bruises, scratches, splinters.

5 Help assemble a first aid kit for home or troop.
OR list ten common household items that must be kept out of reach of small children and tell why.

6 List three or four rules for safe use of playground and camping equipment and tools.

7 Practice what to do if someone's clothes catch fire.

8 Show how you gradually take more responsibility for your health as you grow older. Show this in a play or poster which you and others plan and carry out.

My signature

Leader's signature   Date badge completed

Home Health and Safety

Purpose: To learn and practice safety measures that will protect you and your family.

When you complete a requirement, have leader initial and date it.

1 With an adult in your family, label clearly and arrange neatly the contents of the medicine chest.

OR know and follow proper procedures for use and storage of flammable or poisonous liquids and powders, matches, and medicines found in your home.

2 Learn and practice the safe use of three things commonly used for each of the following: cooking, housecleaning, repairing, playing.

OR select three different kinds of rooms and discuss with others what should be done in each to help keep the family safe and healthy.

3 List five common causes of fire in the home and steps for fire prevention. With your family, plan what you would do if there were a fire in your home.

4 Plan a diorama, peepshow, poster, or skit on home health and safety.

OR make and carry out a health and safety plan for your troop meeting place.

5 Using what you have learned, survey your apartment, house, yard, or farm and list any unsafe conditions. With the help of your family, correct as many as you can.

My signature

Leader's signature

Date badge completed

Hospitality

Purpose: To learn how to be an even better friend, a courteous guest, and a thoughtful hostess.

When you complete a requirement, have leader initial and date it.

1 Talk over with your patrol different ways to make new friends and keep old friends.

2 Explain ways you can be polite and show you really care about another person by the ways you talk and act.

3 List things you should think of and do as an overnight hostess and as a guest. Compare lists.

4 Practice making introductions correctly. Introduce: your Girl Scout leader or teacher to your parents, a new girl to your troop, a boy to a girl friend. Discuss ways to make newcomers feel at ease.

5 Learn how to write a thank you note for a gift or a visit, and a friendly letter to a sick person. Know the parts of a letter. Tell how to address the envelope. Know different kinds of stationery.

6 Put on a skit showing thoughtful telephone manners.

7 Set a table for two kinds of meals. Act out or make a poster about table manners.

8 Discuss a variety of ways to show others you care about them on birthdays and holidays.

9 Using your new ideas and skills, plan and serve nutritious refreshments or give a party for your family, patrol, or other group of friends.

My signature

Leader's signature   Date badge completed

Housekeeper

Purpose: To learn and do the things necessary to keep a home pleasant, clean, and safe.

When you complete a requirement, have leader initial and date it.

1 Find out the cleaning activities that are done in a home. Choose two and help to do them each week.

2 Check the plan in your home for safe storage of cleaning equipment and supplies. Consider space, when and where equipment will be used, convenience, and the safety of young children.

3 Learn how to sort clothes and how they should be laundered. Describe care of your Girl Scout uniform.

4 Keep a record of the money you spend for two weeks. Talk with your family about your expenses and some possible ways to earn money.

5 Do the following: Help clean the refrigerator. Show how to use a broom, dust mop, vacuum cleaner. Demonstrate a good method of dishwashing. Clean the kitchen or bathroom floor, sink, and fixtures. Demonstrate bedmaking. Wash a window. Clean a room thoroughly. Tell why it is important always to turn off lights, faucets, and other fixtures when you finish with them.

6 Organize your closet, drawers, and belongings neatly.

7 Visit grocery stores to compare labels on different food packages. Look for information on quantity, quality, and price.

My signature

Leader's signature

Date badge completed

Indian Lore

Purpose: To learn about the traditional ways American Indians lived in this country.

When you complete a requirement, have leader initial and date it.

1 Know the history of the American Indians from your locality. Describe the Indian homes, dress, and food and tell where the Indian descendants live today.

2 Describe briefly the American Indian tribes or nations who lived in four different parts of the United States: Alaska, Northwest coast, California, Basin-Plateau, Southwest, Great Plains, Northeast, or South. Tell how Indian life was affected by where they lived.

3 Tell which states have names of American Indian origin. Give the meanings of three such state names.

4 Visit an American Indian exhibit in a museum or at a fair.
OR attend an American Indian ceremony or event.
OR talk to an American Indian to learn more about Indian culture today.

5 Tell about the life and contribution of an American Indian heroine or hero.

6 Read at least three American Indian legends. Choose one and tell it to a group of Brownies or other friends.

7 Choose two of the following: Make a useful article and decorate it with an authentic American Indian design.
OR make a model of the traditional American Indian houses of your part of the country.
OR learn to play an American Indian game and teach it to your patrol or troop.
OR show some American Indian dance steps.
OR teach an American Indian song to your patrol, explaining its meaning and how the song was used.
OR make an American Indian musical instrument and use it in camp or at a troop meeting.

My signature

Leader's signature

Date badge completed

Magic Carpet

Purpose: To discover what you can do with stories and books to give pleasure to others.

When you complete a requirement, have leader initial and date it.

1 At a troop meeting tell about a short trip you took and what you enjoyed most about it.

OR describe something that happened to you when you went to camp or visited a relative or a friend.

2 Get your own library card or know how to apply for one. Discuss the responsibilities of having a card.

3 Pick out and read two books. Choose from folk stories, poetry, or books about animals, nature, a different country, or an American heroine.

4 Bring the book you liked best to troop or patrol meeting. Tell why you enjoyed it and read something from it. When other troop members tell about books they liked, make a list of those you would like to read.

5 Read a favorite short story or poem aloud, or prepare a story and tell it as part of a troop meeting or ceremony.

6 Collect at least 12 poems that could be used in troop meetings or for Scouts' Own.

OR select a story and dramatize it with your patrol.

7 Make a jacket for one of your favorite books.

OR start a library shelf or box in your troop meeting place.

8 With others plan a book illustration party at which each troop member sketches a scene from her favorite book.

OR help with a book collection drive in a community or school book project.

My signature

Leader's signature   Date badge completed

Musician

Purpose: To use your musical knowledge for troop, camp, and community events.

When you complete a requirement, have leader initial and date it.

1 Play or sing at sight a simple piece of music. Beat its rhythm and explain all signs and terms.

2 Learn to play alone or with others two accompaniments your troop or fellow campers can dance or sing to.
OR teach an American folk song and singing game.

3 Explain to your patrol what is meant by two of the following musical terms: concerto, quartet, sonata, symphony. Listen to examples of those you have chosen until you can identify them and their composers.

4 Make a simple percussion instrument.
OR explain to others how the instrument you are learning to play is made, how it works, and its range.

5 As a soloist or with others, sing or play background or incidental music for a campfire, Scouts' Own, or other special event.

6 Read the story of an operetta or an opera. Listen to some excerpts from it until you are familiar with them.
OR with others, present a scene from an operetta or opera with friends or puppets and recordings.

7 Write a simple, original tune.
OR listen to a tune and make up dance steps to it.

8 Discuss good concert manners and with others attend a musical event.

My signature

Leader's signature   Date badge completed

My Camera

Purpose: To learn how to use a camera and to take pictures of many things in different lights.

When you complete a requirement, have leader initial and date it.

1 Load your camera with film. After you have finished using the film, unload it. Explain the parts of your camera as you use it or adjust it to take a picture.

2 Make a list of the subjects you plan to photograph. Tell how far away you will stand from each.

3 Show a photograph that tells a story. Explain why it tells a story.

4 Describe how foreground and background objects can help or spoil a picture.

5 Take a time exposure or flash picture.

6 Take a series of pictures of the same subject showing variation in light and shadow: light behind the object, light behind the camera, light from the side, through a doorway or branches, close up, far away.

7 Take pictures to use as a record of a trip or an event.
OR take pictures to tell a story and choose a title for the story.

8 Mount one or two of your best pictures.
OR start a photograph album. Write captions for the pictures.

My signature

Leader's signature   Date badge completed

My Community

Purpose: To find out about your community—its history and the ways it helps the people who live there now.

When you complete a requirement, have leader initial and date it.

1 Find out how your community got started. Visit at least one historic place.

2 Learn when your state was admitted to the Union. Make pictures of your state flag, flower, and bird, and explain why each was chosen. Give your state motto and tell what it means.

3 Visit a newspaper or a radio or television station to learn how they keep your community informed of local, national, and international news. Tell why this is important. Share at least two current events with your troop.

4 Locate on a map and then visit one of the public recreation areas near where you live. Explain who operates this area and why we have such areas.

5 Show how citizens use hospitals, libraries, schools, and social agencies in your community. Explain through a poster, display, skit, or booklet what the community would be like without these agencies.

6 Show how you would help a visitor learn about and see some of the interesting places near you.

7 Take part in a service project that will help your community.

My signature

Leader's signature

Date badge completed

My Home

Purpose: To find ways to make your home a more pleasant place to live.

When you complete a requirement, have leader initial and date it.

1 List the things each family member does to help the others every day, which make your home a pleasant place to be. Discuss things you now do or you might do. Tell which Girl Scouting activities help you to be a better member of your family.

2 Talk or write to older people and learn how they lived at your age and what they liked to do.

3 With a grownup present, play with a small child several times. Read a story with him or her. See what toys the child likes and what care he or she needs.

4 Make something useful for your home such as hand-sewn articles or small household objects.

5 Find out how a girl of your age in another country lives.
OR interest your family in trying a food of another country. Help prepare and serve it.

6 Plant and care for house plants or garden for a month.
OR care for a pet for a week.

7 Plan ways to make a room in your house or apartment more attractive: helping to rearrange furniture, making a schedule to keep it clean, putting up or changing a picture, storing clothes.

8 Discuss some new service you could give in your home and do it.

My signature _____

Leader's signature _____   Date badge completed _____

My Trefoil

Purpose: To discover and practice more ways to carry out the Girl Scout Promise.

When you complete a requirement, have leader initial and date it.

1 Start a scrapbook of poems, quotations, and pictures that illustrate: On my honor—I will try—To serve God—(To serve) my country and mankind.

2 Learn from Girl Scout books a grace to sing and a song for patriotic occasions.

3 Find out about the customs of different religious faiths that affect holidays, food, and activities, so that you can respect the beliefs of all Girl Scouts when planning activities together.

4 Explain how the second part of the Promise—"To serve...my country and mankind,"—is connected with the Girl Scout motto, "Be Prepared," and the slogan, "Do a good turn daily."

5 Watch to see the many things people do to help each other. Make up charades, shadowgraphs, or a skit to show some of the things that you observed and are going to do.

6 Make a list of ways you will try to live up to the Law. Next, write down the Law. Stop and think about everything you did in one day. Then look at the Law and note, beside each part, anything you did that was affected by that part.

OR cut from newspapers and magazines pictures or stories that illustrate each part of the Law, and explain why you chose those pictures and stories.

7 Do one or more service projects that would carry out the Promise.

My signature

Leader's signature

Date badge completed

My Troop

Purpose: To become a better member of your troop so that you can do more for it.

When you complete a requirement, have leader initial and date it.

1 Show that you know how Girl Scouting started in the United States.

2 With your patrol make a chart showing how your troop is a part of its Girl Scout neighborhood, council, region, and national organization. Know the name of your council. Know the states in your region.

3 Explain what the two circles of the patrol leader cord stand for. Explain how you can do your part at patrol meetings and troop meetings.

4 Plan and carry out an opening ceremony and a closing ceremony for your troop.

5 Collect and record dues for your patrol or shop for some troop supplies. Help figure out a budget for a troop event.

6 List people who have helped your troop in the past year. Plan ways to thank them.

7 Do something to improve your troop meeting place or campsite.

8 Show how to wear your Girl Scout uniform and insignia. Explain why you should wear them neatly and correctly.

9 Invite a Cadette to tell you what her troop does.
OR help a Brownie cross the bridge to Junior Girl Scouting.
OR do a Junior Aide Patch requirement.
OR take part in a Girl Scout Week activity.

My signature

Leader's signature   Date badge completed

Needlecraft

Purpose: To learn many different stitches and use them to make or decorate articles you have designed.

When you complete a requirement, have leader initial and date it.

1 Learn four of the following: blanket stitch, chain stitch, cross stitch, French knot, outline stitch, satin stitch. Practice using the stitches by working a picture or sampler.

2 Decorate household articles or pieces of clothing using two or more of the following: crewelwork, crocheting, darning stitch, hemstitching, huckaback darning, needlepoint, needle weaving, smocking stitch.

3 Work out on graph paper a simple design for needlepoint or cross stitch.

4 Make a small design using appliqué, quilting, or hooking.
OR create a picture or design for a wall hanging or pillow cover using stitches learned in No. 1.

5 Display at a troop meeting the things you made.
OR invite some troop members to see your display.

Kim Reinhard

My signature

Leader's signature

Date badge completed

42

Observer

Purpose: To know how and why nature changes with the seasons.

When you complete a requirement, have leader initial and date it.

1 With others, take an adventure hike in a park, zoo, or your neighborhood. Look for: plants, trees, animals, reptiles, amphibians, insects. Look for them in another season. Note the changes.

2 Know a rock formation, three weather signs, and two cloud formations.

3 Find out about noise, air, water pollution, or soil erosion. Make an exhibit showing how your community is affected by these problems.

4 Locate four constellations such as the Big Dipper, Little Dipper, Orion, Cassiopeia. Try to find them at another season of the year.
OR visit a planetarium or an observatory.

5 Plant a flower garden for birds at two different seasons of the year.
OR identify or press fall or spring leaves.
OR choose a small area, watch to see what lives there, and check it at another season for any change. Tell others what you find.

6 Observe two of the following: an ant carrying a load twice its size, a bee getting pollen or nectar from a flower, a bird building its nest, a mud wasp building its nursery, a spider wrapping its prey with its web. Tell others what you have seen.

My signature

Leader's signature   Date badge completed

Outdoor Cook

Purpose: To learn how to build different fires and prepare food with and without fire.

When you complete a requirement, have leader initial and date it.

1 With four to eight other girls, help plan, prepare, and serve four different meals, including four different types of cooking. Help do the following in each meal: plan balanced menus, make shopping list, shop, take care of food at site, establish eating place, prepare and serve food, and clean up.

2 Help set up and use four different types of fireplaces and fires. Explain when to use each type of fireplace and fire. Build and use one fire without adult help.

3 Make a cooking fire for windy or wet weather.

4 Use correct knots to make hanging caches and dunking bags.
OR make shavings and point sticks.
OR make two pieces of outdoor cooking equipment.

5 Have your own cooking kit. Help plan and assemble a patrol cooking kit.

6 Tell about two games that could be played while a meal is cooking.
OR help make a troop or unit outdoor recipe file.
OR select two eatable wild foods.

7 List five ways you have practiced good fire and cooking safety.
OR know first aid treatment for burns and cuts and tell ways such injuries can be avoided.
OR know how to dispose of waste water and garbage without damaging the environment.
OR learn how to sterilize your dishes.

My signature

Leader's signature

Date badge completed

Pen Pal

Purpose: To correspond with a pen pal and learn to write different kinds of letters.

When you complete a requirement, have leader initial and date it.

1 Practice writing the following to a real or imaginary friend: thank you note for gift or visit, letter with news of friends or community, account of a troop or school project, something humorous to amuse a sick friend, invitation to attend a party or to make a visit, letter to a younger or an older person.

2 Share these practice letters with other troop members working on the badge and exchange ideas for making each other's letters more interesting. Ask your parents, teacher, or other adult friend to help you improve the form, punctuation, writing, and neatness of your letters.

3 Correspond with a pen pal—a new friend or one you do not see often. In your letters try to: Find out about her hobbies and tell her about yours. Give her news about your Girl Scout troop. Illustrate at least one letter with sketches, photographs, or pasted pictures and tell her about your family and home. Tell her about one place in your community that you like to visit.

4 Practice wrapping packages securely and neatly. Show that you can address them correctly. Learn how to pack a fragile object. Find out about the different rates for mailing packages.

5 After you have exchanged two or more letters with your pen pal and feel you know each other well, discuss with your leader, patrol, or troop what has made the correspondence interesting.

My signature

Leader's signature

Date badge completed

45

Personal Health

Purpose: To learn how and why to guard your own health.

When you complete a requirement, have leader initial and date it.

1 Have a health examination. Make a record of the doctor's advice and follow it.

2 Make a chart showing foods necessary for a well-balanced diet. Find out how these foods help to build sound teeth and strong bodies. Plan and eat a balanced meal using the basic four food groups.

3 Explain proper care of teeth, hair, skin, hands, and feet.

4 Demonstrate good posture in sitting, walking, standing, and lifting.

5 Know five diseases from which you can be protected by inoculations. Keep a record of the inoculations you have had.

6 Discuss with your troop or patrol why active games and sports are important to your health. Learn and teach an active game to your troop or younger children.

7 Help plan and carry out a program that shows the rules of good health. Use posters, games, skits, songs, exhibits, or plays.

8 Make a chart of the health steps you have learned. Check yourself on the chart for two weeks to see if you can improve your health habits.

My signature

Leader's signature

Date badge completed

Pets

Purpose: To find out more about your pet and how you can look after it.

When you complete a requirement, have leader initial and date it.

1 Read at least two books about your kind of pet. Be able to tell about the history of that kind of animal and others of the same family.

2 Take responsibility for your pet for at least two months, providing it with the right kind of shelter, food, and exercise.

3 Discuss the kinds of illness common to your pet and how you protect it against disease.

4 Know what to do when you see your pet is ill: what precautions to take until help is available, how to get in touch with a veterinarian, how to give your pet medicine if your veterinarian and parents want you to.

5 Tell how a female pet should be cared for before and after she has her young. Learn: the kind of food the newborns need if natural food is not available, the kind of nest or bed needed, and how to housebreak young if they are to be allowed inside. Find out how to prevent pets from having unwanted young.

6 Show the proper way to carry your pet from one place to another safely. If your pet can be trained, know how to give it training directions.

7 OR Know about a society to protect animals. OR visit an animal shelter.

8 Make a record of anything you have or know about your pet: photographs, sketches, shots, special treatments.

My signature

Leader's signature   Date badge completed

Prints

Purpose: To make different kinds of prints for yourself and others.

When you complete a requirement, have leader initial and date it.

1 Collect things with which to make an impression or "gadget" print, such as: bottle caps, dowel ends, eraser, screws, sponge, sticks. Use a stamp pad. Experiment with one item at a time to create a border design, an allover pattern, or a design in two colors.

2 Make a transfer print with leaves, ferns, or bark.
OR make a rubbing of something "raised" or engraved such as: a carving; a design on an iron gate; the texture of a leaf, bark, brick, or stone.

3 Make a stencil using your own design. Show safe way to use a stencil cutting tool. Paint your stenciled design on paper or fabric.

4 Make a relief print. Either cut your design in an eraser, linoleum, potato, soft wood, or glue a felt, rubber, or cardboard design to a wooden or heavy cardboard block. Print your design on paper or fabric.

5 Show a greeting card you like and tell how it was printed. Find examples of prints from different countries and times in history, or make a scrapbook of different kinds of prints and label each one.

6 Print a wall hanging, a picture, a decoration on an article of clothing, or a bookplate.

My signature

Leader's signature   Date badge completed

Rambler

Purpose: To discover some of the secrets of nature.

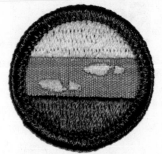

When you complete a requirement, have leader initial and sign it.

1 Go on walks or hikes with family or friends and make a list of the different places where you find wildlife. Observe two of the following: animals gathering food, creatures that live under rotting logs or loose boards, insect moving its mouth parts, moths or butterflies laying their eggs.

2 Identify four or more migrating birds as they pass through your area in the spring or fall.
OR make up a game that uses pictures of birds.

3 Use a magnifying glass to explore a seashore or the edge of a stream, pond, or lake. Write down your discoveries or make a collection of some of the nonliving objects to exhibit.

4 Make a plaster cast of an animal track.
OR develop a short nature trail and guide illustrating at least ten objects to look for along the way.

5 Tell how to recognize and avoid poisonous plants. Know what to do if you brush against them.

6 Take a nature walk in the woods or an arboretum. Look for plants, ferns, mosses, lichens, cacti, and similar things common to your part of the country.
OR be able to identify three different plants or trees in your area.

My signature

Leader's signature   Date badge completed

Sewing

Purpose: To start to sew and make something you can use.

When you complete a requirement, have leader initial and date it.

1 Collect equipment for a personal sewing box. Include shears, pins, needles, thread, tape measure, pincushion, thimble. Learn sizes and kinds of needles and thread you need and the proper way to use sewing tools.

2 Find at least six different kinds of fabric or visit a store that sells fabric. Compare the way different fabrics feel. Find out which can be washed and which must be dry cleaned.

3 Make two items: something to wear, something for your home or meeting place, or something to be used on a camping trip.

4 Look at pattern books. Choose a pattern you would like. Discuss fabrics you might use.

5 Name the parts of a sewing machine. Show how to thread it and run it. Practice stitching evenly.

6 Do the following: Make plain seams. Finish seams by pinking, overcasting, edge stitching. Show running, hemming, overcast stitching. Hem, fringe, or bind an edge. Sew on snaps, hooks and eyes, and buttons. Prepare fabric for cutting.

7 List ideas for future sewing you would like to do for yourself, your home, a gift, and a service project.

My signature

Leader's signature   Date badge completed

Skater

Purpose: To learn how to be a good roller skater or ice skater.

When you complete a requirement,
have leader initial and date it.

1 Tell how to select and care for skates. Explain safety rules for roller skating or ice skating. Show how to stop quickly.

2 Using good form, skate forward, backward, to your left, to your right, around corners to the left, and then to the right.

3 With a partner, skate forward, backward, and in a dance position.

4 Learn to play and teach one skating game.

5 Practice skating to music and be able to do one dance to music.

6 Explain or show how to give first aid to a skater who is hurt. Explain how to rescue an ice skater who has fallen through the ice.

7 Read about ice skating or roller skating. Be able to discuss the diet, exercise, and training required for a champion skater. Be able to recognize advanced styles of skating.

8 Help plan and take part in a skating party either indoors or out.
OR make and wear part of a safe skating outfit.

My signature

Leader's signature

Date badge completed

Songster

Purpose: To learn many songs for different occasions.

When you complete a requirement, have leader initial and date it.

1 Sing well with a group the following: a folk song, art song, round, or canon. Know the source of each song you select and some interesting information about each.

2 Make a list of songs for opening and closing troop meetings, ceremonies, hiking, and special days at camp. Know how to sing these songs.

3 Sing a program of typical songs of the United States.
OR plan and perform a song program for a national holiday.

4 Tell a legend or folk tale about which a song or other musical composition has been written.

5 Make up actions to go with a song.
OR invent a game using music.

6 Plan and give a program based on the songs and life of a famous composer.
OR plan and give a program on the folk songs of one country, and be able to tell interesting facts about that country's history, customs, and special contributions to the world.

My signature

Leader's signature

Date badge completed

Storyteller

Purpose: To read, listen to, and make up stories to tell or read to others.

When you complete a requirement, have leader initial and date it.

1 Read ten different kinds of stories out loud to yourself. Keep a card file of stories you think are good to tell. Make a note on each card of where you found the story, the time it takes you to tell it, and the age group that would enjoy it.

2 Watch a good storyteller and her listeners to see what she does to add to the interest of the story. Discuss what makes a storyteller interesting and why people like to listen to a good storyteller.

3 Find or write a story about a place you have traveled. Tell it to your troop or camp group.

4 Find in a dictionary the definitions of some words you do not know. Learn to pronounce them and use them correctly.

5 Practice telling several stories from your file to a friend or your patrol. Select the one you do best and tell it to a larger group.

My signature

Leader's signature   Date badge completed

Toymaker

Purpose: To make toys or games for children.

When you complete a requirement,
have leader initial and date it.

1 Choose an age group of children for whom you want to make toys or games. Find out what kinds of toys those children enjoy. Explain which toy materials are safe to use and why.

MAD

2 Bring to a troop meeting samples of toys and games to help you decide what you want to make.

3 Practice on scrap materials, using tools you will use to make the toys or games.

4 Spend four or more meetings or afternoons helping to make or repair toys or games.

5 Check the toys or games you have made to be sure they are completely finished and that any necessary directions have been included.

6 Help wrap and pack the toys or games to give to the children.

Kim Reinhard

My signature

Marlee Dorman

Leader's signature

_3/2/81_

Date badge completed

Troop Camper

Purpose: To learn and practice the things you need to know to go troop camping.

When you complete a requirement, have leader initial and date it.

1 Help your troop plan and carry out a trip to a cabin, cabin unit, or cottage for at least two nights. Help plan where, when, and how to go; what to take and wear; what to do; what permissions are needed. Know something about the site, what is provided there, and how best to care for it. Help plan the expenses.

2 Help plan suitable meals. Make food lists. Secure, pack, carry, store, prepare, and serve food. Clean up. Plan and cook one meal outside.

3 Use a kaper chart that gives each girl a turn at different camp jobs.

4 Know how to make a bedroll or tie up your sleeping bag. Dress for the expected weather and for the activities you have planned. Have your equipment well tied together.

5 Plan or be responsible for one of the following activities on the weekend: activities for weather that keeps you indoors, evening program, flag ceremony, grace for a meal, hike, nature trail, outdoor game, outdoor good turn. Plan equipment needed.

6 Help plan times for getting up in the morning and getting settled at night, times for meals and for rest.

7 Help check the troop first aid kit. Talk about emergencies that may occur and what to do about them.

8 Help settle in at the site and, when you leave, help put the site in good condition.

9 After the trip, talk over how the trip went and what you would do differently next time.

Kim Reinhard
My signature

_____
Leader's signature

Date badge completed

55

Troop Dramatics

Purpose: To know the first steps in acting and putting on plays.

When you complete a requirement, have leader initial and date it.

1 With your patrol, act out three ideas in which you see, hear, taste, feel, or smell. Have your troop discover what you are acting out.

2 Make up a sentence and say it in different ways to show such feelings as: surprise, alarm, sadness, happiness, fright.

3 Help plan a ceremony to welcome fly-up Brownies or other new members to your troop.

4 Learn four basic acting terms that will help you on stage.

5 Make up a play about a story from a Girl Guide country.
OR help dramatize an incident from Juliette Low's life.
OR dramatize a historical event or legend connected with your community.

6 Find out what choral reading is. Prepare two readings for a troop ceremony, a campfire, or a parents' meeting.

7 Go to see a play at a school, church, or community theater. Discuss what you learned at the performance that would be useful in putting on a troop play.

8 With your patrol or others, read together two or three plays or stories that could be dramatized. Pick one and decide who will act, make scenery, and make costumes. Present your play to a troop or other group.

My signature

Leader's signature   Date badge completed

Water Fun

Purpose: To carry out a variety of activities near and in the water.

When you complete a requirement, have leader initial and date it.

1 Demonstrate that you can float for one minute. Swim ten meters (about ten yards). Demonstrate that you can do two different strokes. Tread water for one minute.

2 Without going in the water, demonstrate how to use a towel, pole, or other object to help a tired swimmer. Explain why the buddy system is good to use wherever you swim. Discuss safety around water.

3 Demonstrate how to get into and out of a boat safely. Learn and practice putting on a personal flotation device correctly. Tell why it is important to wear a personal flotation device in a boat. Show you can row a boat or paddle a canoe.

4 Read a story or learn two songs about the sea, lakes, or rivers.

5 By, on, or in the water, do two of the following: Draw, paint, or photograph life on or near the water. Have a campfire, Scouts' Own, or other ceremony. Have a picnic or cookout. Play two water games. Sail model boats. Visit a boatyard, fish hatchery, aquarium, or water life museum.

My signature

Leader's signature   Date badge completed

Weaving and Basketry

Purpose: To learn about and practice different kinds of weaving and basket making.

When you complete a requirement, have leader initial and date it.

1 Look for five types of weaves. Collect swatches or pictures and display them.

2 Weave a small sampler, mat, or purse on a cardboard loom or other type loom. Use two or more colors. Try different types of weaves and textures.

3 Make a tee dee loom or a flat frame loom and demonstrate how to use it.
OR use a simple harness loom and experiment with different textures and colors. Make a belt with finger weaving or some other simple type of weaving.

4 Find examples, collect pictures, or make sketches of different kinds of basketry. List the different materials and colors used.

5 Experiment with natural dyes for your weaving or basketry materials.

6 Investigate natural materials in your community that could be used for basket making without disturbing the environment. Gather fibers and prepare them for use.

7 Make a basket. Use any of the methods you have learned.

My signature

Leader's signature   Date badge completed

World Games

Purpose: To learn, play, enjoy, and be able to lead games played around the world.

When you complete a requirement, have leader initial and date it.

1 Choose six Girl Guide/Girl Scout countries. Find and play one game from each country. Discuss why children from the country play that game.

2 Discuss safety precautions that need to be taken when playing games with others.

3 Play and be able to lead four of the following kinds of games: action game for children younger than yourself, circle game, get-acquainted game, nature game, paper and pencil game, quiet game, relay, stalking game, tag game, testing game, wide game. Include at least one international game.

4 For a play day with your troop or other group, be able to lead and participate in one team sport or one skill game.
OR help make some troop game equipment.

5 With your patrol adapt three games for convalescent or handicapped children.

6 With your troop or patrol plan a world games party and invite another troop or patrol to it. Have an exhibit of books with games from other countries.

My signature _____

Leader's signature _____ Date badge completed _____

World Neighbor

Purpose: To know more about how other children in the world live.

When you complete a requirement, have leader initial and date it.

1 Tell your troop about *Trefoil Round the World* or *The Council Fire*, published by the World Association, which tell about Girl Guides and Girl Scouts in other countries. You may borrow these from your leader or council office.

2 Explain what the World Association of Girl Guides and Girl Scouts is. With your troop learn and sing "The World Song."
OR tell something about each of the four World Centers. With your troop learn and sing "Our Chalet Song" or "Our Cabaña Song."

3 Make a scrapbook about children on four different continents. Collect pictures or make illustrations of their towns, cities, homes, schools, plants, trees, animals, dress, or food.
OR learn and sing one song from another country.

4 Find out about organizations that help children around the world. Tell your troop about the organizations.

5 Take part in a project for children in another country. See *Unravel the World*, pages 28-31, for ideas for projects.

6 Learn to say at least "hello" and "good-bye" and to count up to ten in two languages other than English. See *Say It in Another Language* for ideas.

7 With your troop or patrol plan: how to welcome persons from another country and what to show them, how to communicate with them if they don't speak English easily, and what you might learn from them. Prepare a booklet for your visitor that shows how children live in your part of our country.

My signature

Leader's signature   Date badge completed

Writer

Purpose: To try different kinds of writing so you will know more about being a writer.

When you complete a requirement,
have leader intial and date it.

1 Jot down in a notebook ideas you would like to write about. Write at least 150 words about one of them. Share what you have written with your patrol.

2 Help prepare four issues of a troop newspaper with: news, feature stories, reports of meetings, notice of future events, and interviews.

3 Correspond with a friend or relative about what you enjoy most in Girl Scouting.

4 Write a poem giving your thoughts or feelings about something or someone.

5 Write a story or short play for your patrol to act out for your troop or other group.

6 Choose a favorite legend or folk tale and write it as a puppet show or a play.

7 Write a report of some of your troop activities for your council, sponsoring group, or school bulletin.

8 Find out how a writer's manuscript is turned into a printed book.

My signature

Leader's signature   Date badge completed

Our Own Troop's Badge

When you and other members of your troop have an interest that is not included in any of the badges in this book you can develop a special Our Own Troop's _____Badge on that subject. An individual girl cannot do this badge by herself. A group must make up the requirements, the name, and the symbol together. No other girls in your troop or in any other troop can use your badge. Even if they choose the same subject, they must create their own requirements and symbol.

To earn this badge:

Make sure that your chosen subject is not covered in any of the Junior badges, and that it does not conflict with the Girl Scout Promise and Law.

Ask your council for approval of your badge subject. The council approves only the subject of the badge, not its requirements.

With your leader, review the meaning and characteristics of Junior badges. Then write your own requirements on the next page, agree on a name for the badge and a design for the badge symbol. The name of your subject goes in the blank space in the title Our Own Troop's_____Badge. Each girl puts the badge symbol the troop has designed on her own blank badge with the green border.

Do the requirements in a way that satisfies yourselves, your leader, and your consultant (if you have one for this badge).

When you have completed your badge, send a copy of the requirements and a sample of the cloth badge you designed to your Girl Scout council office and to Program Department, Girl Scouts of the U.S.A., 830 Third Avenue, New York, N.Y. 10022. People in these places want to keep up with new ideas from troops, and they might decide to put your badge on display.

Our Own Troop's _____ Badge

When you complete a requirement, have leader initial and date it.

Purpose:

1. _____

_____

_____

_____

_____

_____

_____

_____

_____

_____

_____

_____

_____

_____

_____

_____

_____

_____

_____

My signature

_____

Leader's signature   Date badge completed

Signs of a Junior Girl Scout

A Junior Girl Scout may earn the Sign of the Arrow and the Sign of the Star. Each of the two Junior Girl Scout signs has its own symbol that you can wear on your uniform sash as a reminder of your adventures and accomplishments.

The requirements for the signs are different from those for a badge. A badge is about one subject, while a sign includes *many different* subjects to explore. Like badges, signs have requirements to help you get started. For some parts of a sign you might even choose to earn a badge.

There are two ways to earn each of the Junior Girl Scout signs—the *traditional* way and the *new* way. With your leader's help compare them and decide which way you like the best.

Sign of the Arrow

The Sign of the Arrow is a symbol of direction and discovery. It gives you, as a Girl Scout, the chance to find and follow many paths to fun, learning, and adventure. A girl wearing the Sign of the Arrow has gained new skills and can set new directions for herself.

Most girls will earn the Arrow first. But you do not have to earn the Arrow in order to work on requirements for the Star. You can work on either one that the girls of your age are working on when you join the troop.

The Traditional Way to Earn the Sign of the Arrow

Complete all nine activities in any order to earn the Sign of the Arrow.

1 Earn a badge that teaches you something you can use on hikes or cookouts or in exploring the out-of-doors.

I earned the   badge.

2 Each of the country's symbols has a story to tell. Find out about some of these symbols and tell your troop about one of them. Find out how to care for our country's flag. Help plan and carry out a flag ceremony. Look in *Worlds to Explore* handbook for information.

Symbols I know

I told my troop about

Date of flag ceremony

3 Earn a badge about cooking or sewing or being a hostess or looking after your room or yourself.

I earned the   badge.

4 Find out how to greet Girl Guides from other countries in their own language and practice the greetings (see *Say It in Another Language*). Explain the symbol of the World Association as it is shown on the World Association pin (see *Worlds to Explore* handbook).

Greetings I learned

I explained the World Association pin to

5 Earn a badge about one of the arts—music, dancing, dramatics, literature, painting, or crafts.

I earned the _____ badge.

6 Help plan and take part in a Scouts' Own.

Theme of Scouts' Own: _____

7 Take part in a service project with your patrol or troop.

I helped _____

8 Get together with another troop or camp unit to meet new girls and to do something together.

We got together with _____

What we did: _____

9 Take part in a Girl Scout project that Girl Scouts all over the United States are taking part in, or one that all Girl Scouts in your town are taking part in.

Project: _____

Date Sign of the Arrow completed _____

My signature _____

Leader's signature _____

The New Way to Earn the Sign of the Arrow

To earn the Sign of the Arrow the new way, choose and complete at least two activities in each of four action areas.

The four action areas are:
Going Places
Making Things Happen
Building Friendships
Helping Your Community

The activities you do may be different from anyone else's because you choose those which interest you most and figure out how you will do them. When you have completed activities for each of the four areas, you can receive the Sign of the Arrow as a bright symbol of your accomplishment.

Going Places

Around the corner or around the globe, the world is filled with interesting things and people. You can open the doors of discovery with a little curiosity and alertness.

Test your know-how for finding your way by doing at least two of these activities:

Take a trip with friends or family to some place near or far—some place you have never been before. Help decide where and how to go, and what you will see and do there and on the way.

Keep some kind of log or record of your trip, which you can save and share with others. Include your thoughts and feelings about what you saw and did.

I visited _____ on _____

I went with _____

OR earn a badge that helps you learn something you can use during hikes, camping, or other outdoor activities, or for exploring your community.

Decide Guide: What would you like to learn?
What badges might help you learn these things?

I earned the _____ badge,

because _____

The most interesting thing I learned was _____

OR take part in a project that helps you learn something about girls and boys your age who live in another part of your community, another part of the United States, or another part of the world.

Decide Guide: Whom do you want to learn about?
What do you want to find out?
What kind of project could help you find out what you want to know?

I learned about

The kind of project I took part in was

OR create and carry out your own Going Places project, different from any of these — a project you design to help you explore your special interests in people and places.

The project I (we) created was

Some discoveries I (we) made

Making Things Happen

Putting ideas in action is what Making Things Happen is all about. Working with others to make your ideas become reality is how it's done. Have the fun of sharing and learning as you make your ideas count.

Do at least two of these activities:

With your patrol or others in your troop, plan and rehearse an entertainment you could put on at short notice. Choose an audience and put on your entertainment, then be ready to perform again if you should be asked.

Our entertainment was about

It was held at   on

We put on our entertainment for

and again for

OR help plan and carry out a skills day, play day, or song festival.

Decide Guide:　　When and where will you hold it?
　　　　　　　　What games, songs, or activities will you include?
　　　　　　　　Who will be invited and how will you invite them?
　　　　　　　　How much will your program cost?
　　　　　　　　How will you pay for your program?

We held a

that took place on

We invited

OR with others in your troop, choose a subject you want to learn more about. Invite someone who is an expert on that subject to visit and teach you some of the things you want to know about or learn to do.

Decide Guide: What interests you most?
What Whom will you invite?
What will you ask this person to do?
When and how will you invite your guest?

The subject we chose was

We invited

who is an expert on

What we most enjoyed doing was

Some things we learned by carrying out our project were

OR with two or three friends, invent something that can be used and enjoyed by all members of your troop—a secret code, a game, or anything else you think they could use or would enjoy. When your invention is completed, share it with the troop and tell them how each inventor helped create it.

We invented

I helped by

OR with others, create and carry out a special Making Things Happen project that is different from any of these—a project that helps you and your friends put your own ideas into action and make them count.

The project we created was

What we made happen was

Building Friendships

Help yourself discover more about making, keeping, and being a friend.

Do at least two of these activities:

Reach out to make a new friend by getting acquainted with someone whom you would like to be friends with. Together, do some things that help you and your new friend get to know each other better.

Decide Guide: Whom would you like to be friends with?

What interests do you share and what new things could you learn?

What kinds of things would be fun for you and your new friend to do together?

My new friend is

How we first met was

OR help plan and take part in a project that helps Brownie Girl Scouts learn something about being a friend-maker.

Our project was

What I helped the Brownies learn was

What I learned about making friends is

OR design and make a gift that someone you know could use and would enjoy. It might be for a friend your age, or for an adult who is important to you.

I decided to make

for

because

OR help a friend do something that he or she thinks is very important.

I helped my friend to

How I helped my friend was

OR create and carry out your own special Building Friendships project, different from any of these — a project that helps you make new friends or strengthen old friendships.

The project I created was

What I learned about friendship is

Helping Your Community

Simply living in a community makes you a member of that community. By actively involving yourself in its problems and projects you have an effect on the kind of place your community is. Try making yourself count as a citizen.

Do at least two of these activities:

Make up a game to help people learn interesting things about your community. Teach your game to as many different people as you can.

My game helps people learn more about

I shared my game with

OR help create and carry out a project that demonstrates how Girl Scouting helps your community.

Decide Guide: What do people in your community already know about Girl Scouting?

What more would you like them to know?

What are some ways you can show how Girl Scouts help as members of the community?

I worked with

What we did was

OR help a community group or organization that is doing something to improve your town. Use your skills to carry out some part of the effort.

Decide Guide: What are some community projects girls your age might help with?
What kinds of help can you offer?
How will you arrange to take part in the project you choose?

The group I helped was

How I helped was

Some things I learned about being an active citizen are

OR develop and carry out your own special Helping Your Community project that is different from any of these—a project that involves you in your community.

The project I (we) developed was

What I (we) learned about community action is

OR earn a badge that helps you learn something about being a good citizen in your home, in your troop, in your school, or in your neighborhood.

Decide Guide: What do you think a good citizen needs to know and do?
What badges might help you to learn or do some of these things?

I earned the _____ badge,

because _____

_____

Date Sign of the Arrow completed _____

My signature _____

Leader's signature _____

Sign of the Star

A star shines in all directions and guides you along the way.

Exploring, seeking, and testing are all important parts of the Sign of the Star. Earning this sign helps you look at yourself, other people, and the world in new ways. You are called upon to act on your new discoveries to help your world and to become the kind of person you would like to be.

As you work toward the Sign of the Star, think about the part of the Girl Scout Law you are following. Talk it over with troop members when you complete each activity.

The Traditional Way to Earn the Sign of the Star

Do all seven requirements in any order to earn the Sign of the Star.

1 An alert citizen knows her way around town. Do one of the following: Take a trip to some place in your town you have not visited before.
OR tell someone how to reach places you have visited and what there is to see there.

What I did was
_____

2 Earn a badge on preventing accidents or one on health care.

I earned the _____ badge.

3 Do one of the following: Attend a Girl Scout camp. Go camping with your troop. Go day camping.
OR earn one out-of-doors badge.

What I did was
_____

4 Take part in a program that includes stories or songs or games about at least one of the following: Juliette Low's Birthplace, National Center West, Olave House, Our Cabaña, Our Chalet, Rockwood Girl Scout National Center, Sangam. The program can be a campfire or a Thinking Day program or entertainment for a visitor who has been to one of these places.

Our program was about
_____

5 Earn a badge that either gives you a new hobby or tells you more about a hobby you already have. At a troop meeting, share what you learned by showing something you made or by explaining something you learned.

I earned the _____ badge.

I told _____ about it.

6 Be a hostess. Help plan and take part in a program that shows other people what your troop does. Use the skills you have learned in making invitations and decorations. Help with the food, planning, or entertainment.

What I helped with was _____

_____

7 Take part in a service project with your troop or patrol.

What I helped with was _____

_____

_____
Date Sign of the Star completed

_____
My signature

_____
Leader's signature

The New Way to Earn the Sign of the Star

To earn the Sign of the Star the new way, choose and complete the activities for each of six Action Calls.

The six Action Calls are:
Discovering You
Getting Things Done with Others
Improving Your Community
Communicating
Being Creative
Choosing Ideals

With your troop leader's help, plan and carry out each project. When you have met all six Action Calls you can proudly say, "I have earned the Sign of the Star."

Discovering You

Most everyone is interested in how things work: why it rains, how an engine runs, or what makes an animated character move around a screen. To find out, you can read and ask questions, but often the best way to understand something is to experience it. The same is true when it comes to understanding the way you work. Self-discovery can often be as simple as taking a step back and watching yourself in action.

Do at least two of these activities to help discover more about yourself:

Teach someone else how to do something that you can do well—something that would be useful or enjoyable to the other person.

OR list three or four things that are especially hard for you to do, and choose the one most important to you right now. Find some ways to learn to do it better.

OR create something that tells others about yourself. You might make a painting, collage, or photo collection, write an original story or poem, or do something different from any of these ideas. Make your choice, carry it out, and share your original creation with your family and troop.

OR invent some ways to become a better friend, student, or family member. Test your ideas and, if you aren't satisfied, make changes to improve your plan. Invent an interesting way to share your discoveries with your troop.

Explore:	Who and what are important to me?
	What can I do well?
	What would I like to learn, try, or practice?
Seek:	In what ways can I share my knowledge, skills, and talents?
	What are some people, places, things to do, that can help me learn something?

Getting Things Done with Others

Experience the feeling of team spirit and accomplishment that comes from working with others to choose and reach a common goal.

Do any one of these activities:

With a group, create your own newspaper. Name it and share the responsibility among yourselves for gathering information, putting it all together, and getting it to your readers.

OR with others in your troop, create an Our Own Troop's Badge.

OR with others, choose, plan, and carry out three "Secret Good Turns" for someone else.

OR with members of your family, choose, plan, and carry out a special project that all of you would like to do together.

Explore:	What actually happens when a group of people plan and carry out a project together? What was easy and fun about it? What was difficult about it?
Seek:	What are ways of choosing and planning that are fun for everyone in the group? What is a project that we will be proud of?
Test:	How well can I work as a member of a group to get something done? How can I use what I learn to plan and carry out other projects?

Improving Your Community

City or suburb, town or country village, your community—like your troop—is only as great as you make it. As a citizen, you have responsibility for your community, as do your parents and others younger and older than yourself. Look around. Are there things that need doing? Be an active citizen. Don't wait for someone else to get things going— make your move!

With your patrol or another group, choose, plan, and carry out a project to help make your community a better place to live.

Explore: What is "best" about our community?
How do people live, work, and grow in it?
How could it be improved?
How can we find out about these things?

Seek: What are the most useful things we can do for our community?
What are some ways of doing these things?
Who can help us carry out our plans?
What skills do we need to carry out our plans?

Test: How well do we plan together?
What happened as a result of our efforts?
Was our project a success, or could it have been more effective?
What changes would we make if we did it again, and what would we do the same?

Communicating

Words, pictures, and movements are a few of the many means of communicating. Even when you don't realize it, you are sending out and receiving messages.

Increase your knowledge and skill in communicating by doing at least two of these activities:

Make up your own play, comic strip, chart, movie, or filmstrip about troop government and how it works. Present and discuss this with a group of Brownie Girl Scouts, younger or new Junior Girl Scouts.

OR meet with a girl your own age who is a member of an ethnic, racial, or religious group different from your own. With her, develop a project or activities that you can do together to help each of you learn more about your likenesses and differences.

OR go on a silent communications search. Explore some ways that people can "talk" to each other about themselves and about ideas and feelings *without using words*. Try some ways of silent communication yourself and share your discoveries with your family or troop in some interesting way.

Explore: How do people communicate with others?
Seek: In what ways can I sharpen my skills of communicating ideas, thoughts, and feelings?
            What happens when people can communicate with each other?
            What happens when people can't communicate with each other?
Test: How well can I communicate with people, older and younger, similar to and different from myself?

Being Creative

Cooking a tasty meal, solving a problem, or organizing an enjoyable project—creativity is an important part of so many things. By pooling your experience, imagination, and ingenuity with others, you can combine ideas to come up with something that is new and exciting.

With others, make up a wide game (see *Worlds to Explore* handbook) that can help members of your troop discover more about each of these things:

listening and observing,

solving a problem,

creating a story, skit, picture, or poem.

Explore: Why do people like to play games?

What makes a game interesting? exciting? dull? useful?

Seek: What kinds of activities help people learn more about how to listen? to solve problems? to use their skills and talents?

How do we go about planning an activity for someone else to do? What things do we have to think about?

Test: Can we put our ideas together so our game is fun for everyone?

What did we learn by planning the game?

What do we think others learned by playing the game?

Choosing Ideals

Everyone chooses ideals to live up to. Where do ideals and values come from, and how do you decide which ones are important to you?

Begin your own ideals quest by doing at least two of these activities:

Start a collection of pictures, stories, and poems that tells about the different ideals and values that people have and about how they try to live up to those ideals in their daily lives.

OR create a play for a Scouts' Own, or a TV show, film, or filmstrip about the Girl Scout Promise and Law and what they mean to you.

OR choose two or three people in your community whom you admire—people living by ideals you think are important. Plan and carry out an interview with one of these people. Decide what questions you will ask in the interview and how you will record the conversation.

Explore: What are some examples of ideals and values?
              How do people express their ideals and values?

Seek: What is important to me?
              What are my ideals?
              How are they different from or similar to ideals of other people?

Test: How well do I act on what I believe?
              How can I live up to my highest ideals?

_____

Date Sign of the Star completed

_____

My signature

_____

Leader's signature